CONSTANCE MILLER'S

Floral Book
of Days

CONSTANCE MILLER'S

Floral Book of Days

DOUBLEDAY
New York London Toronto Sydney Auckland

Published by Doubleday, a division of Bantam
Doubleday Dell Publishing Group, Inc.
666 Fifth Avenue, New York, New York 10103

Doubleday and the portrayal of an anchor
with a dolphin are trademarks of Doubleday,
a division of Bantam Doubleday Dell Publishing
Group, Inc.

First published in Great Britain 1988 by Webb &
Bower (Publishers) Ltd. in Association with Michael
Joseph Ltd. as *Constance Miller's Book of Flowers*.
First published in Australia 1988 by The Macmillan
Company Ltd. as *Constance Miller's Book of Flowers*.

ISBN 0-385-26267-1
Text and illustrations copyright © M. J. Cummins 1988
Biographical Introduction by Cathryn Game

CONSTANCE MILLER

1 8 7 9 - 1 9 6 8

Constance Miller was born in California on 1st October 1879. She came from a staunch English family background. She never married. Her father was highly protective of his daughters and rejected any suitors he considered not worthy of them. So she devoted herself to her closely knit family and to the Anglican church.

Such an existence may sound limited by today's standards, but Constance's life was full and interesting. It was also pleasant and gracious as the family had private means from both her father's and her mother's sides. Constance had an active mind and, like the rest of the family, strong Christian principles. She read and wrote many letters to friends and family both in Australia and England. These letters sparkle with her great zest for life and unfailing good humour. Her main personal interests were painting, embroidery and poetry; she also taught at Sunday School and wrote plays for the children of her sister's school. She never had a paid career, but was involved in many charitable works and was deeply interested in education. She was closely involved with the Girls' Friendly Society, and even visited England with a GFS group. With her mother and sister she was a co-foundress of Western Australia's first Mothers Union Branch at Fremantle.

In 1905 Constance painted a birthday book illustrated with Western Australian wildflowers and presented it to the State Governor, Admiral Sir Frederick George Denham Bedford, and his wife. Her friends urged her to do another one, and it is this book which is now published for the first time. It contains 113 Western Australian wildflowers painted in watercolours. Each flower has been depicted accurately and given its botanical name. It was lent to Government House for the visit of Queen Elizabeth II and the Duke of Edinburgh in 1954. The *Western Mail*, describing the rooms to be occupied

by the royal couple, said, 'An interesting West Australian touch to the suite will be given by an old-fashioned birthday book containing wildflower paintings, which will be lying on one of the tables'.

Constance Miller's father, Frederick, was born in London in 1849. His father, Taverner John Miller, was Conservative Member of Parliament for Colchester from 1857, during Disraeli's prime ministership. Frederick was educated at Westminster School and learned to play Westminster Abbey's organ. When he was eighteen he went to Australia and New Zealand for a visit. He married Constance Mary Sumner in 1872, in a village church in the Cotswolds near the Sumner family home in Gloucester. Through her mother, Constance was descended from John Bird Sumner, who became Archbishop of Canterbury in 1848, and her great-grandfather was Bishop of Winchester and Dean of St Paul's Cathedral.

The couple lived at Southsea for about three years, where their first child, Marian, was born. Frederick had two yachts and won several prizes in Cowes Regattas. In 1875, the Millers sailed for California to join their relations Fred and Cecil Sumner on their ranch near Los Angeles. They stayed for about seven years. Three daughters were born there, Dora (who died when she was three), Constance and Rosalie. When Rosalie was a few weeks old the family returned to England, where sons Hubert and Fred were born. Then, on 31st October 1889, the Millers sailed for Australia in the *Wilcania*. After a voyage of forty-two days, stopping only in Las Palmas, the ship anchored in Gage Roads and the passengers — the first to arrive by steamer — were brought ashore to Fremantle in lighters.

The Millers spent their first few months, including Christmas, in the Cleopatra Hotel in Fremantle, until Frederick rented a small farm of eighty hectares, eight kilometres south of Fremantle. The house, Woodlands, had been empty for years. Cows and horses had made a mess of it, and the rooms had to be dug out and scrubbed. Water came from a well with a hand-pump. The family spent seven years there and it was an exciting time. Gold was discovered in the region and camels used for transport were quartered in paddocks near the Miller's home. The horses were terrified and the camels ate and completely destroyed the beautiful surrounding bushland. Hindu and Afghan camel drivers fought each other in their camps and the Miller family were often asked for medical assistance.

When Marian's husband, Frank Lodge, bought Chepstowe, a house on the riverfront at Peppermint Grove, Perth, in 1895, the Frederick Millers decided

to move nearby. They rented a large house, Mozaphir. Marian opened a junior school, which thrived, and Hubert built his house next door. Five years later, the Frederick Millers moved to Hesslemount, another stately house in Peppermint Grove.

Frederick senior lived the life of a Christian gentleman, spending every Friday morning at his club in Perth and playing the organ at the local church. He used to compose settings for the 'grace before meat'. The family would sometimes gather at the top of the staircase, then walk down the stairs into the main hall singing the grace in four parts while their father played the harmonium in the hall.

In 1897, the Miller family were instrumental with other Anglican residents of Peppermint Grove in building the Parish of St Luke's. Long before the foundation stone was laid, a choir began practising at the Miller home with Mr Miller as choirmaster and organist. Mrs Miller had an extra practice for the boys she had enlisted each week after school hours. The walk to St Luke's was mostly through the bush as there was only one hard road in the suburb. As the church was nearing completion, a Sunday School was started, a tent being provided for this purpose. On the first Sunday, no seats had arrived for the students. Nothing daunted, teachers and scholars stood for the lesson. Constance remembered her feelings facing her class as a teacher for the first time: 'I was young, and had never taught anyone before (there was no "commission to teach" in those days), but my parents had taught me and my terror soon vanished.'

In those days it was the custom for whole families to go to church together every week and St Luke's was a happy meeting place for friends. Constance writes: 'and did we sing!'

An amusing story she relates is about the first resident clergyman (1899):

'A tall young Irishman, then only a deacon, he wore a tall hat and frock coat, even when riding a bicycle in summer. He knocked at one door, and enquired in his soft Irish voice, "Do you belong to me?" but the lady of the house answered, "No, I don't. I belong to my husband," and the door banged in his surprised face.'

Fred, Constance's brother, and his nephew, Frank Lodge, took up and cleared a farm, Quarabin, at Babakin about 250 kilometres east of Perth. They then both enlisted in the Australian Imperial Forces in 1916. Constance composed a farewell poem for them, and two farming friends from Babakin, presenting it to them at a large party in the family home before they left:

Now come all ye dancers and come neighbours all
I have a toast to propose
There are four gallant bushmen just off to the War
Good fellows as everyone knows.
So fill up your glasses, their good health to pledge
They are Percy and Freddie and Frankie and Reg . . .

Yes fill up your glasses and cheer up your cheer
And shout as you ne'ere did before
And give them a send off they'll never forget
These gallant young soldier boys four
For "Bedar" and "Quarabin" will feel a great blank
Without Regie and Percy and Freddie and Frank.

Then fill up your coffee cups, cocoa and tea
And wish them the best of Good Luck.
For they're four bonza Bushmen wherever they be
Full of courage and muscle and pluck.
We'll cheer them and sing them with song and with verse
Young Frankie and Regie and Freddie and Perce.

And when we have cheered them — as in Days of Yore
Crusaders went gallantly off to the war
We, like their well loved ones left lonely behind,
Will pray for them, think of them, keep them in mind,
And welcome them Home again when wars are sped
Old Percy and Regie, and Frankie and Fred.

Fred was killed at Noreiul on 2nd April 1917 and Frank at Passchendaele on 12th October 1917. In 1920 Constance and her mother went to England and France to visit their graves. In a typewritten, eleven-page letter Constance relates their experiences. Leaving the family home at Gloucester, they crossed the Channel from Dover to France and spent a few days with friends at Wimereau on the coast near Boulogne, before going on to Lille and the battle areas. With them was an English relative and a Major Cobb who helped them find the graves. Army officers and an Australian sergeant from Perth working in wooden huts at Duisans gave the party a map and in the next couple of days they travelled through the former battlefields. Constance's spirited and good-humoured account never falters, although clearly she was moved by what she saw:

'We reached Noreiul, which consists of a few little huts and . . . the Major found what is probably the very spot where Fred was killed. It is now a field, looking so calm and peaceful in the sunshine, and while we stood there a lark rose quite near us, singing as hard as he could. I took two photos . . . and we came away feeling so happy to have seen it all looking so bright and peaceful . . .'

They continued through France into Belgium the next day. Constance took a lively interest in all she saw and in the people she met. At Passchendaele the party had to abandon their car and walk through swampy soil and shell craters — which were filled with water even at the end of summer — to reach the cemetery. They put daisies and cornflowers on Frank's grave and took photos before having tea with the Captain in charge of the British headquarters nearby. After a couple more days Constance and her mother returned to Gloucester, 'feeling our visit to France had been one of the wonderful experiences of a lifetime'.

In 1924 Mrs Miller began to build Home Cottage — named after her sister's home in England — in Forrest Street, Peppermint Grove, but she died before it was finished. It was Constance's home for the rest of her life.

Constance made extended visits to her brother Hubert's sheep and cattle station, Yandal, which was about 1,000 kilometres north-east of Perth. It was a property of 155,501 hectares. In 1927, for example, she stayed for three months. In that time she wrote a steady stream of brisk letters to her sisters and to her nieces who were visiting relatives in England. Their letters back to Constance evoked happy memories of her own visits to England — 'woods, hills, bluebells, cowslips, thrushes and distant views' — and she responded with vivid descriptions of station life:

'Fencing by contract is going on both east and west, which will mean two huge new paddocks (she wrote on 23rd April 1927). Boring for water is the order of the day for this section of the men folk, the feed is very good everywhere, but more rain is needed to bring the 'winter herbage' to perfection so I don't expect I shall see many flowers, as I must go home again in June, and the flowers will not now be earlier than usual, vis: Sept.'

Later in the same letter:

'Next Monday and Tuesday are great days in Darlot! The cricket match and race meeting. The city of Darlot consists of one pub, and not much else! McRobertson's station homestead is just outside the city walls and luckily they have invited us to

spend two nights with them or we should have to camp out, the pub being impossible. We have to go to the races!! . . . The races were to have been held on Monday and the cricket match on Sunday — then it was discovered that Monday was Anzac Day, so of course a race meeting could not be held, as it ranks as Sunday. Evidently the pub is not quite so much needed for a cricket match! Quite a large meeting is expected, 75 programmes have been ordered!!!!! Nellie (Hubert's wife) and I are taking our best dresses and are looking forward to plenty of interesting experiences!'

Then a couple of paragraphs later, Constance describes the pivotal role of the station car, 'Lizzie':

'"Lizzie" is truly wonderful! She is just the busiest little car anywhere! She does anything and everything. Dashing off with campers kit, a load of fencing posts, half a bullock lying on the back seat, meat for the contractors, and then takes beautiful ladies in their best dresses to the races, all with the utmost good will and cheerful 'whirr', just as busy as she can be. The station would be lost without "Lizzie".'

Members of the family remember Home Cottage and their great-aunt Constance Miller fondly. Tall and thin — 'her back was so straight you could have put a ruler down it; she used to wear a straw hat with a scarf from the crown tied under the chin when she collected flowers from the garden, basket in hand'. Meal times at Home Cottage were proper and formal, with linen and silver settings. Grace was said before and after meals.

Hubert came to live with Constance, and with Annie Baldwin, the house-keeper of many years, after his wife had died and Yandal was sold in 1955. Constance and Hubert were devoted to each other. Constance would spend Saturday afternoons sitting on the lawn at the yacht club watching him sail. It was one of her favourite spots, in the cool sea breeze under huge pine trees. On hot evenings they often had tea on Hubert's anchored yacht.

Sunday was a family day. Church was followed by a roast lunch, and in turn by an elaborate, old-fashioned afternoon tea, with scones and cakes and tea in a silver teapot. Sometimes there were family picnics in the bush or, in September, visits to King's Park, which Constance loved, to see the wildflowers.

When Constance Miller died in July, 1968, she closed a chapter of life of enduring values, lived amid great change and turmoil. She is fondly remembered and respected by all who knew her.

The

Western Australian

Floral

Birthday Book

1912

By

C. Miller

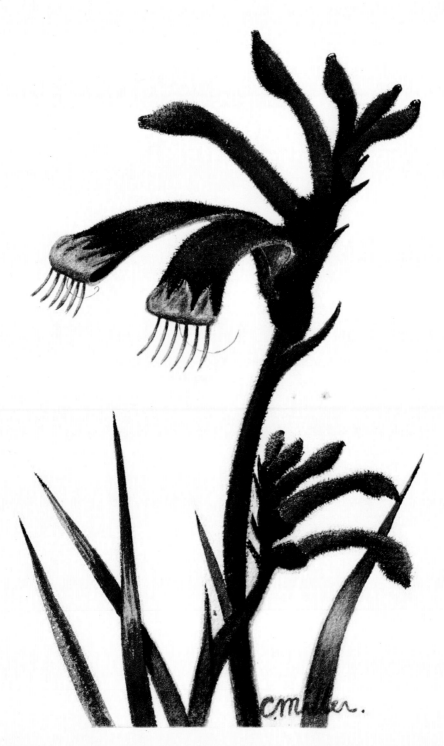

Anigozanthos Manglesii.

Full many a flower is born to blush unseen

And waste it's sweetness on the desert air.

Gray.

January

As half in shade, and half in
    sun,
This world along its path
    advances,
May that side the sun's
    upon,
Be all that e'er shall meet
    thy glances

Moore.

Grevillea Thelemanniana

1

2

3

4

January

It's guid to be merry and wise,

It's guid to be honest and true.

Burns

And thus he bore without abuse,

The grand old name of gentleman.

Tennyson.

Adenanthos barbigerus.

5

6

7

8

January

I held it truth with him who sings

To one clear harp in divers tones,

That men may rise on stepping-stones

Of their dead selves, to higher things

Tennyson.

Grevillea bipuinatifida.

9

10

11

12

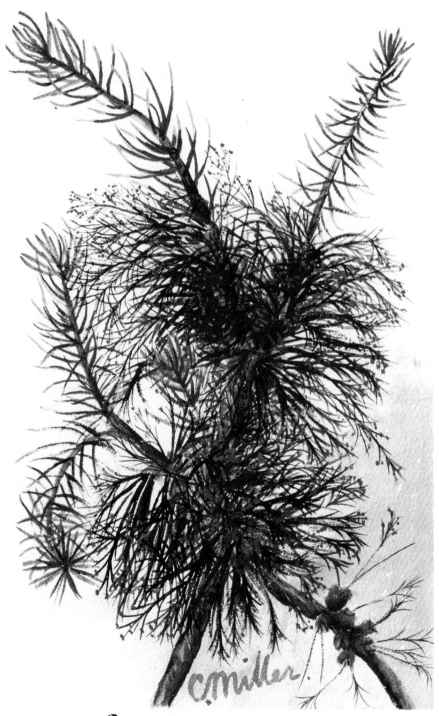

C.miller.

Calothamnus quadrifidus.

14

15

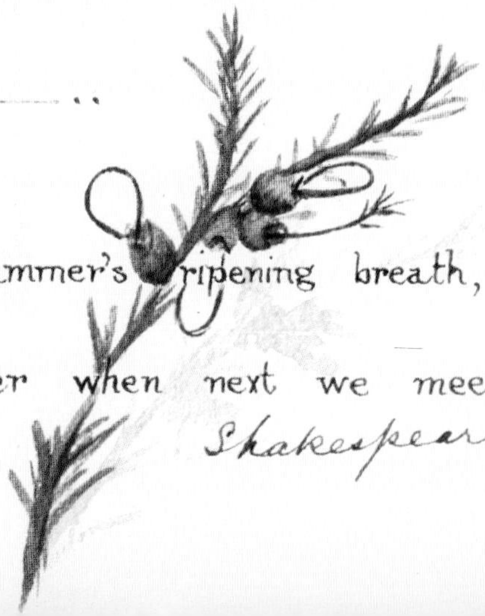

This bud of Love by Summer's ripening breath,

May prove a beauteous flower when next we meet.

Shakespeare.

January

Peace be around thee, where'er thou rov'st,

May life be for thee one summer's day;

And all that thou wishest, and all that

thou lov'st,

Come smiling around thy sunny way.

Moore.

Grevillea Wilsoni.

16

17

18

19

January

So many worlds, so much to do,

So little done, such things to be.

Tennyson.

What's brave, what's noble,

Lets do it. *Shakespeare.*

C.M.

Glory Pea.   Clianthus Dampieri

20

———————————

21

———————————

22

———————————

23

January

Every man has a sane spot somewhere.

Stevenson.

What tho' care killed a cat, thou

hast mettle enough in thee to kill care.

Shakespeare.

Leschenaultia formosa.

24

25

26

27

January

A perfect woman nobly planned,
To warn, to comfort and command.
Wordsworth

And I will say, as still I've said,

Though by ambition far misled,

Thou art a noble knight.
Scott.

Kennedya prostrata.

28

29

30

31

Anigozanthos   humilis.

February

1

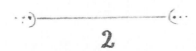

2

The best of happiness

Honour and fortunes, keep with you.

Shakespeare.

Cyrtostylis reniformis.

February

But in spite of all temptations,

To belong to other nations,

He remains an Englishman!
Gilbert & Sullivan.

To be what we are, and to

become what we are capable of becoming,

is the only end of life.
Stevenson.

Caladenia discoidea.

3

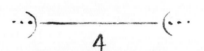

4

5

6

February

How far that little candle throws his

beams!

So shines a good deed in this naughty world.

Care to our coffin adds a nail no doubt,

And every grin so merry

draws one out.

Dr. Walcot.

Verticordia nitens.

7

8

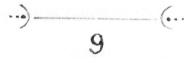

9

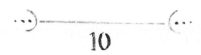

10

Oxylobium capitatum.

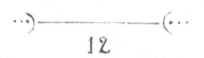

12

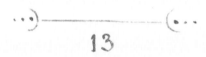

13

He that would climb a tree, must grasp by the branches, not by the blossoms.

Darwinia citriodora.

February

Dwells within the soul of every Artist,

More than all his efforts can express;

And he knows the best remains unuttered,

Sighing at what we call success.

Procter.

She is as noble-hearted as she is beautiful.

Dickens.

Leschenaultia linarioides

14

15

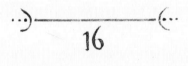

16

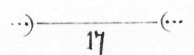

17

February

"Man is his own star; and the soul that can

Render an honest and perfect man,

Commands all light, all influence, all fate,

Nothing to him falls early or too late.

Our acts our angels are, or good or ill,

Our fatal shadows that walk by us still."

Hibbertia stellaris.

18

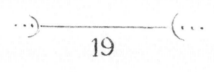

19

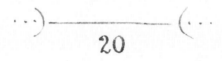

20

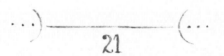

21

February

On the choice of friends
Our good or evil name depends.
      Gay.

A sudden thought strikes me, let
us sware an eternal friendship!
      "The Antijacobin."

I have been there, and still would go,
'tis like a little heaven below.
      Watts.

Isotropis striata

22

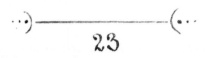

23

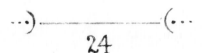

24

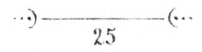

25

February

Of blessings too, I have my store,

Yet quarrel not, should God send more.
Edward Moore.

I only ask that Fortune send,

A *little* more than I shall spend.
O. W. Holmes

A light heart lives long.
Shakespeare.

26

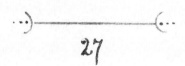

27

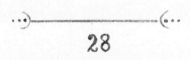

28

29

Kennedya Comptoniana.

March

1

2

3

There is sweet music here that softer falls

Than petals from blown roses on the grass.

Gyanostegia angustifolia

Tennyson.

March

A smiling look she had, a figure slight,

With cheerful air, and step both quick

and light;

— — — — — — — — — —

— the blue fearless eyes in her fair face,

And her soft voice, told her of English

race.

Procter.

Ionidium calycinum.

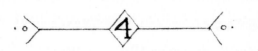

MARCH

Half light, half shade,

She stood, a sight to make an old man

young.
                                    Tennyson.

You talk as if you were an old man,

I never heard such a fellow.
                                    Dickens.

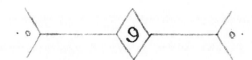

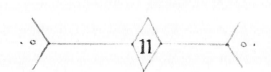

Brachycome iberidifolia.

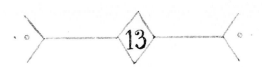

Swans sing before they die - 'twere no bad thing,

Should certain persons die before they sing.

Thelymitra ixioides.

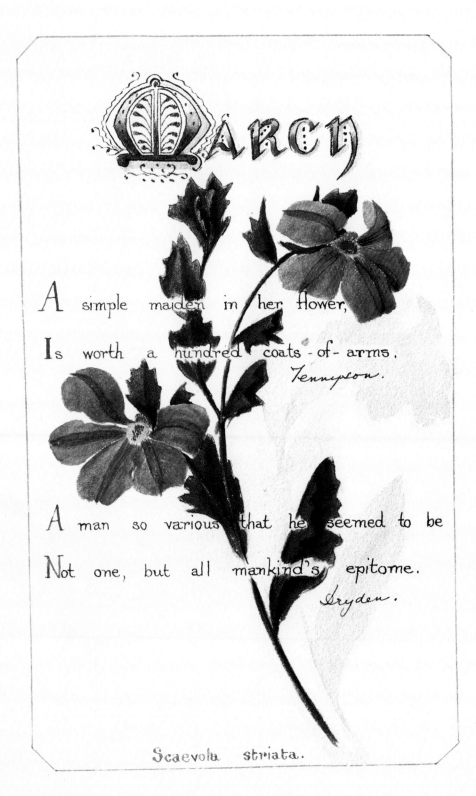

March

A simple maiden in her flower,
Is worth a hundred coats-of-arms.
Tennyson.

A man so various that he seemed to be
Not one, but all mankind's epitome.
Dryden.

Scaevola striata.

MARCH

Talk no more of future gloom:

    Our joys shall always last.

For hope shall brighten days to come,

    And mem'ry gild the past.

Light may come when all looks darkest,

Hope hath life, when life seems o'er.

                    Moore.

Agrostocrinum stypandroides

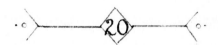

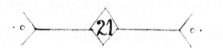

March

He, only, in a general honest thought,

And common good to all, made one of

them.

His life was gentle; and the elements,

So mix'd in him that Nature might

stand up,

And say to all the world "This is a man."

Shakespeare.

Sowerbaea laxiflora.

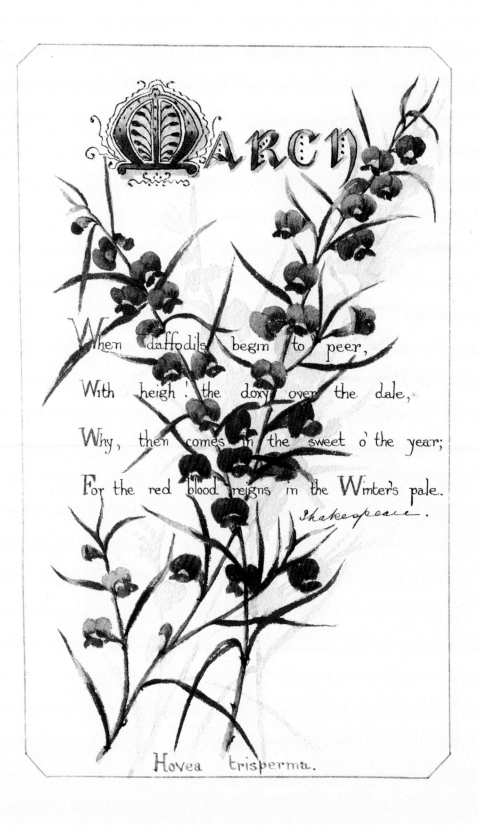

MARCH

When daffodils begin to peer,

With heigh! the doxy over the dale,

Why, then comes in the sweet o' the year;

For the red blood reigns in the Winter's pale.

Shakespeare.

Hovea trisperma.

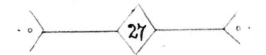

Leschenaultia   biloba.

April

1 _____

2 _____

3 _____

Many years of deserved happiness are,
I trust, before you.

Scott.

April

Everything is possible for him who possesses courage, and activity, and to the timid and hesitating everything is impossible because it seems so.

Scott.

Be bolde, be bolde, and everywhere, Be bolde.

Spenser.

Brunonia australis.

4

5

6

7

April

There's music in the sighing of a reed;

There's music in the gushing of a rill;

There's music in all things, if men had ears;

Their earth is but an echo of the spheres.
Byron.

Of a truth, she is not one to be forgotten.
Scott.

Trachymene caerulea.

8 ———————————————————— 3·

9 ———————————————————— 3·

10 ———————————————————— 3·

11 ———————————————————— 3·

Thelymitra crinita.

12. ⸻ ꒰

13. ⸻ ꒰

14. ⸻ ꒰

⸻

Who hears music, feels his solitude

Peopled at once.

Browning.

Lobelia.

April

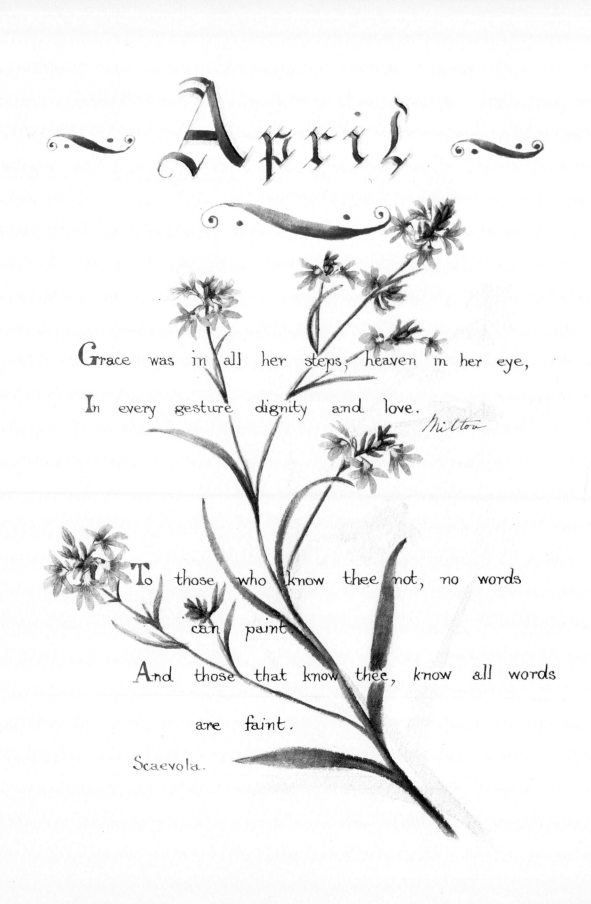

Grace was in all her steps, heaven in her eye,

In every gesture dignity and love.

Milton

To those who know thee not, no words

can paint.

And those that know thee, know all words

are faint.

Scaevola.

15 ———————————————————— 3 .

16 ———————————————————— 3 .

17 ———————————————————— 3 .

18 ———————————————————— 3 .

April

With aching hands and bleeding feet,

We dig and heap, lay stone on stone;

We bear the burden and the heat

Of the long day, and wish 'twere done.

Not till the hours of light return,

All we have built do we discern.

Matthew Arnold.

Scaevola.

19.

20.

21.

22.

April

Should chilling winds and rains come on,

   We'll raise our awning 'gainst the shower.

Sit closer till the storm is gone,

   And smiling, wait a sunnier hour.

And if that sunnier hour should shine,

   We'll know its brightness cannot stay;

But happy, while 'tis thine and mine,

   Complain not when it fades away.

                  Moore.

Linum marginale.

23 _____ 3.

24 _____ 3.

25 _____ 3.

26 _____ 3.

April

Life, exempt from public haunts,

Finds tongues in trees, books in the running brooks,

Sermons in stones, and good in everything.

Shakespeare

How full of briars is this working-day

world.

Shakespeare.

Sollya heterophylla.

27 ——————————————————————————— 3.

28 ——————————————————————————— 3.

29 ——————————————————————————— 3.

30 ——————————————————————————— 3.

Patersonia occidentalis

May

1

2

3

The buds that are longest in blossoming, will
last the longest in flower.

Scott,

Verticordia. pennigera.

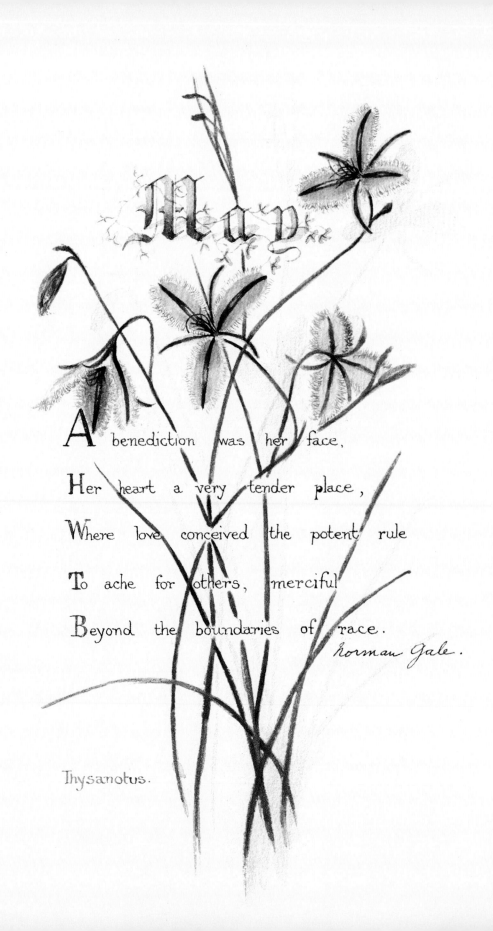

May

A benediction was her face,

Her heart a very tender place,

Where love conceived the potent rule

To ache for others, merciful

Beyond the boundaries of race.

Norman Gale.

Thysanotus.

May

Sing - sing - music was given,

To brighten the gay and kindle the loving;

Souls here, like planets in Heaven,

By harmony's laws alone are kept moving.

Moore.

Platytheca galioides.

9

10

11

12

May

I know thou art what the world calls a brave fellow, and I have ever found thee an honest one.

Scott.

Fair be all thy hopes,
And prosperous be thy life in peace and war.
Shakespeare.

Glossodia Brunonis.

13

14

15

16

Burtonia scabra.

17

18

19

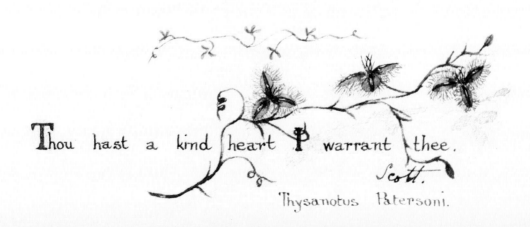

Thou hast a kind heart I warrant thee.

Scott.

Thysanotus Patersoni.

May.

A heart as soft, a heart as kind,

A heart as sound and free,

As in the whole world thou canst find,

That heart I'll give to thee.

Eriostemon spicatus.

20

21

22

23

May

I do love

My country's good with a respect more tender,

More holy, and profound, than mine own life.

Shakespeare.

And then the World arose and said,—

Let added honours now be shed

On such a noble heart and head.

Procter.

Hemiandra pungens.

24.

25

26

27

May

I've often wished that I had clear,

For life, six hundred pounds a year,

A handsome house to lodge a friend,

A river at my garden's end.

Swift.

Calythrix

28

29

30

31

C. milbu

Hypocalymma robustum.

June

1

2

3

A good turn never goes unrewarded.

Scott.

Gompholobium.

June

We live in deeds, not years; in thoughts,

not breaths;

In feelings, not in figures on a dial.

We should count time by heart-throbs.

He most lives

Who thinks most, feels the noblest, acts

the best.

Bailey.

Glossodia emarginata.

4

5

6

7

June

The other side of every cloud

Is bright and shining;

I therefore turn my clouds about,

And always wear them inside out

To show the lining.

May saints and angels bless you.

Scott.

Tetratheca.

8

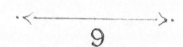

9

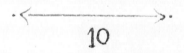

10

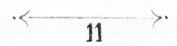

11

Stylidium reduplicatum.

13

14

Man, in the sunshine of the world's new spring,

Shall walk transparent like a holy thing.

Moore.

Trichinium Manglesii.

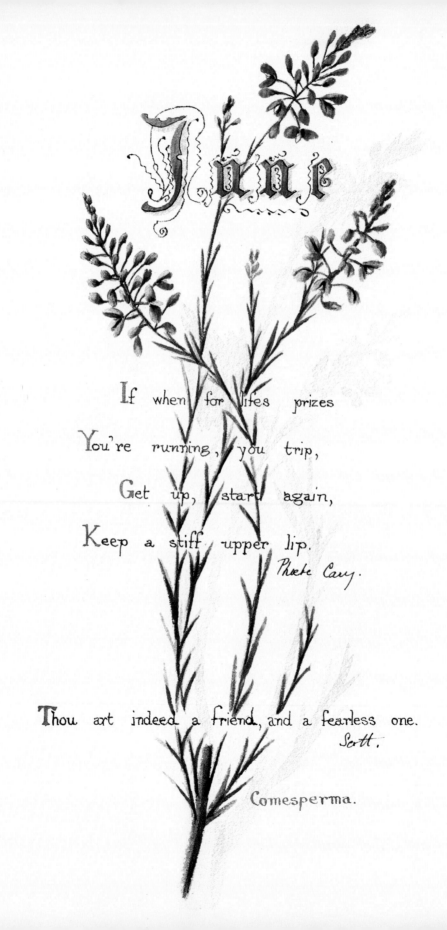

June

If when for lifes prizes

You're running, you trip,

Get up, start again,

Keep a stiff upper lip.
                    Phœbe Cary.

Thou art indeed a friend, and a fearless one.
                    Scott.

Comesperma.

15

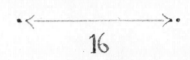

16

17

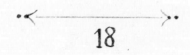

18

June

She *was* a cheerful little thing; and had a quaint, bright quietness about her, that was infinitely pleasant.

Dickens.

You have the character of a young man of sense and generosity.

Scott.

Andersonia.

19

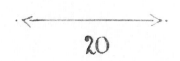

20

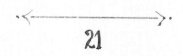

21

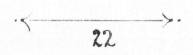

22

June

You've got a very pretty voice, a
very soft eye, and a very strong memory.
                                    Dickens.

The courteous mien, the noble race,
The stainless faith, the manly face.
                                    Scott.

Claytonia limiflora.

23

24

25

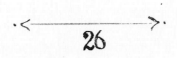

26

June

To see her is to love her,

And love but her for ever;

For Nature made her what she is,

And never made anither
Burns.

He is a man of mirth-ful speech
Can many a game and gambol teach.
Scott.

Melaleuca

27

28

29

30

Candollea.

July

~~~~~~~ 1 ~~~~~~~

~~~~~~~ 2 ~~~~~~~

~~~~~~~ 3 ~~~~~~~

~~~~~~~

The sweetest thing that ever grew,

Beside a human door.

Wordsworth.

Stackhousia

July

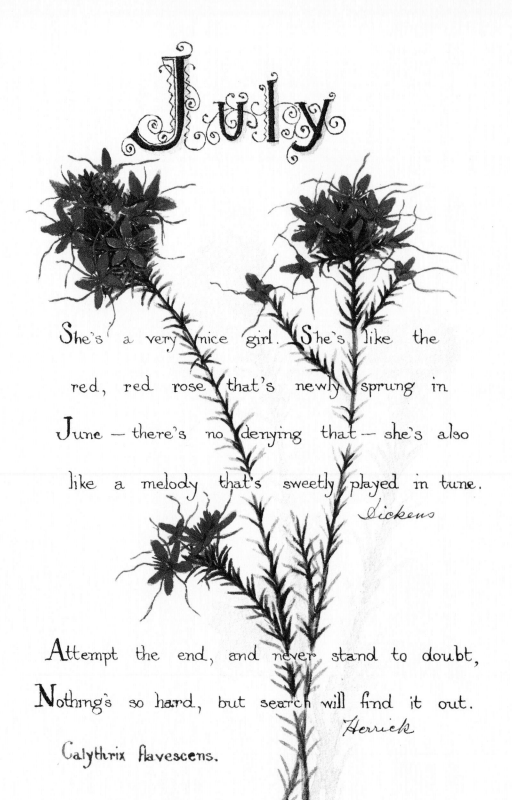

She's a very nice girl. She's like the red, red rose that's newly sprung in June — there's no denying that — she's also like a melody that's sweetly played in tune.

Dickens

Attempt the end, and never stand to doubt,
Nothing's so hard, but search will find it out.

Herrick

Calythrix flavescens.

4

5

6

7

8

July

Love is eternal,

Whatever dies, that lives, I feel

and know—

It is too great a thing to die.

Henry Taylor.

Begin, be bold, and venture to be wise.

Cowley.

Thelymitra antennifera.

9

10

11

12

July

A countenance in which did meet,

Sweet records, - promises as sweet.
Wordsworth.

By the kindness of her ways

She made sweet the sourest days.
J. Piers.

Caladenia flava.

13

14

15

16

Hibbertia hypericifolia.

17

18

19

A garland for the hero's crest,
And twined by her that he loves best.
Scott.

Stylidium.

July

The best of men, the kindest of men,
and yet a man of such admirable strength
of character.

　　　　　　　　　　　　　　Dickens.

The means that heaven yields
must be embraced,
And not neglected.

　　　　　　　　　　　　　　Shakespeare

20

21

22

23

July

Sae true his heart, sae smooth his speech,

His breath like caller air;

His very foot has music in't

As he comes up the stair.
                    Mickle.

If to her share some female errors fall,

Look on her face, and you'll forget them all.
                    Pope.

Thelymitra fusco-lutea

24

25

26

27

July

To thine own self be true

And it must follow, as night

the day,

Thou canst not then be false

to any man. *Shakespeare.*

Gompholobium aristatum.

28

29

30

31

Calectasia cyanea.

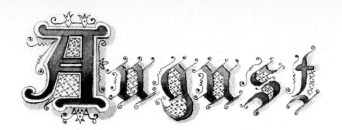

August

1

2

3

Next to enjoying happiness ourselves, is
the consciousness of having bestowed it on others..
Scott.
Caladenia deformis.

August

There is no land like England

Where'er the light of day be;

There are no maids like English maids

So beautiful as they be.

Dampiera linearis.

4

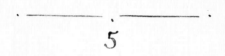

5

6

7

8

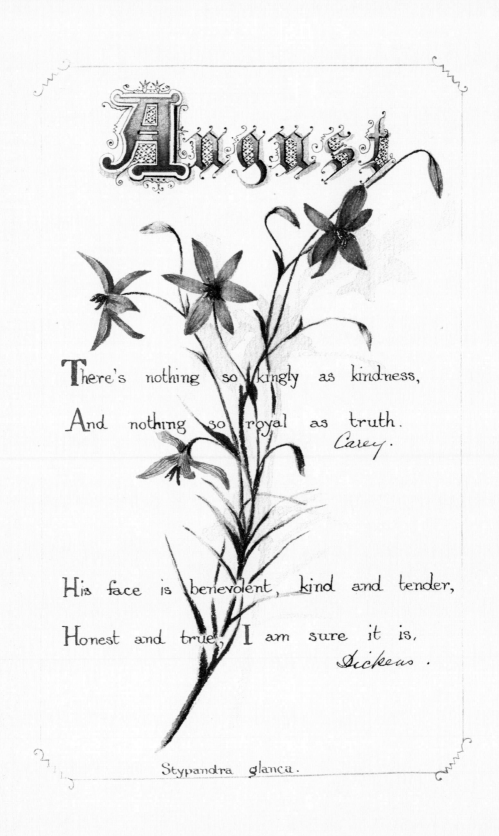

August

There's nothing so kingly as kindness,

And nothing so royal as truth.
                                    Carey.

His face is benevolent, kind and tender,

Honest and true, I am sure it is.
                                    Dickens.

Stypandra glauca.

9

10

11

12

August

The virtue of her lively looks

Excels the precious stone;

I wish to have none other books

To read or look upon.

Boleyn.

Marianthus.

13

14

15

16

Caladenia sericea.

18

19

It was his daily way

To be most gentle both of word and deed,

And ever folk would seek him in their need,

Nor was there any child but loved him well.

Marianthus Drummondianus Morris.

August

She smiles and smiles and will not sigh

While we for hopless passion die;

Yet she could love, those eyes declare,

Were but men nobler than they are.

Matthew Arnold.

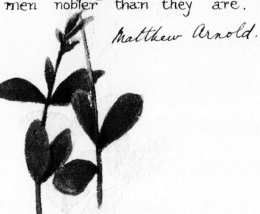

Comesperma.

20

---·--------------·----------------·---
21

---·--------------·----------------·---
22

·--------------·----------------·
23

August

There's something good in all weathers,
If it don't happen to be good for my
work today, its good for some other
man's today, t'will come round to me
tomorrow.

Dickens.

Caladenia gemmata.

24

25

26

27

August

She doeth little kindnesses,

Which most leave undone, or despise;

For nought that sets one heart at ease,

Or giveth happiness and peace,

Is low esteemèd in her eyes.
                                    Lowell.

God bless you, wise and true-hearted man.
                                    Scott.

Lobelia tenuior.

28

29

30

31

Eucalyptus macrocarpa

September

1

2

3

Let fate do her worst, there are relics of joy,

Bright dreams of the past, which she cannot destroy.

Stylidium. Moore.

September

Self-reverence, self-knowledge, self-control,

These three alone lead life to sovereign power.

Tennyson.

Good name in man and woman,

Is the immediate jewel of their souls.

Shakespeare.

Caladenia latifolia.

4

5

6

7

September

I have always heard you mentioned

as a man of wisdom and intelligence,

I have known you myself as a man

of a resolute and independent spirit.

Scott.

Pimelea rosea.

8

9

10

11

September

I live for those that love me,

For those who know me true;

For the Heaven that smiles above me,

And awaits my spirit too;

For the cause that lacks assistance,

For the wrong that needs resistance,

For the future in the distance,

And the good that I can do.

B. Barton.

Diplopeltis Huegelii.

·12·

·13·

·14·

·15·

Verticordia. insignis

·16·

·17·

·18·

My crown is in my heart, not on my head;

Not deck'd with diamonds and Indian stones,

Nor to be seen: my crown is call'd content.

Shakespeare.

Boronia ovata.

September

Proud was his tone, but calm; his eye

Had that compelling dignity,

His mien that bearing haught and high,

Which common spirits fear.
                    Scott.

Stylidium Brunonianum.

—•19•—

—•20•—

—•21•—

—•22•—

September

One by one the sands are flowing,

One by one the moments fall;

Some are coming, some are going;

Do not strive to grasp them all.

Hours are golden links God's token,

Reaching Heaven; but one by one

Take them, lest the chain be broken

Ere the pilgrimage be done,

Procter.

—•23•—

—•24•—

—•25•—

—•26•—

September

The life of all that's good

Is one perpetual progress. Every thought

That strengthens, purifies, exalts a mind,

Betters the soul so blessing.

Bailey.

Drosera macrantha.

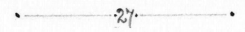

·27·

·28·

·29·

·30·

Verticordia Grandiflora.

October

1

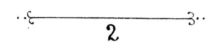

2

3

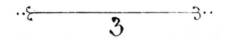

The sky of this life opens o'er us,

And heaven gives a glimpse of blue.

Pterostylis barbata.

Moore.

October

My mind to me a Kingdom is,

Such perfect joy therein I find;

As far excels all other bliss

That earth affords, or grows by kind.

Though much I want, which most would have

Yet still my mind forbids to crave.

Dyer.

Pterostylis recurva.

4

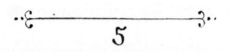

5

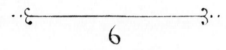

6

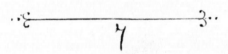

7

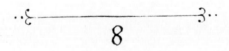

8

October

Though stars in skies may disappear

And angry tempests gather:

The happy hour may soon be near

That brings us pleasant weather.
                                    Burns.

Caladenia multiclavia.

9

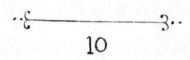

10

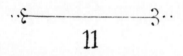

11

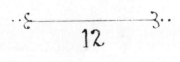

12

October

Conquer we shall, but we must first contend;

'Tis not the fight that crowns us, but the end.

Herrick.

Loving she is, and tractable, though wild;

And innocence hath privilege in her

To dignify arch looks and laughing eyes.

Wordsworth.

Diuris longifolia.

13

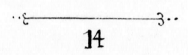

14

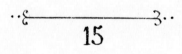

15

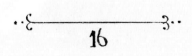

16

Boronia megashgma.

17

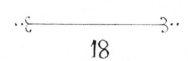

18

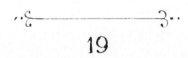

19

This little flower, that loves the lea,

May well my simple emblem be;

It drinks heaven's dew as blithe as rose

That in the Kings own garden grows.

Drakaea elastica

Scott.

October

Music, which gentlier on the spirit lies,

Than tired eyelids upon tired eyes.
                                        Tennyson.

His high endeavours are an inward light,

That makes the path before him always bright.
                                        Wordsworth.

Cryptostylis. ovata.

20

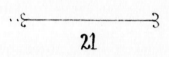
21

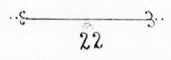
22

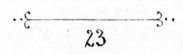
23

October

My heart leaps up when I behold

A rainbow in the sky:

So was it when my life began;

So is it now I am a man;

So be it when I shall grow old,

Or let me die!

The child is father of the man;

And I could wish my days to be

Bound each to each by natural piety.

Wordsworth.

Pterostylis reflexa.

24

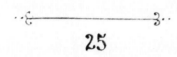

25

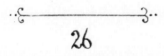

26

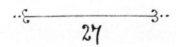

27

October

The powers aboon will tent thee;

Misfortune sha'na steer thee:

Thou'rt like themselves sae lovely,

That ill they'll ne'er let near thee.

Burns.

Diuris longifolia.

28

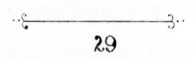

29

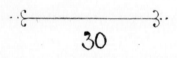

30

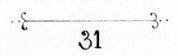

31

Verticordia grandis.

November

1

2

3

One of those bright, bewitching little creatures,

Who, if she once but shyly looked and smiled,

Would soften out the ruggedest of features.

Kunzea.

Pollock.

November

Here's a sigh to those who love me,

And a smile to those who hate,

And whatever sky's above me

Here's a heart for every fate.

Byron.

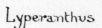

Lyperanthus nigricans.

4

5

6

7

November

A merrier man

Within the limits of becoming mirth,

I never spent an hour's talk withal.

Shakespeare

Your Majesty's reign will need no such feeble aid,

to make it remembered to the latest posterity.

Scott.

You have a good deal of intelligence

for a little fellow.

Dickens.

Caladenia filamentosa.

8

Edward   the   Peacemaker.   1841 - 1910

9

10

11

November

We have not wings, we cannot soar;

But we have feet to scale and climb,

By slow degrees, by more and more,

The cloudy summits of our time.

Longfellow.

Chorizema. Dicksonii

12

13

14

15

Kungea Barteri

16

17

18

Poor Wisdom's chance

Against a glance

Is now as weak as ever.

Caladenia Menziesii. *Moore.*

November

Which do you love best —
  Green leaves, or brown;
Those which in Autumn
  Come fluttering down. —
Those are like old friends,
  Green leaves, like new,
I love old friends best,
  Say do not you?

Caladenia filamentosa.

19

20

21

22

November

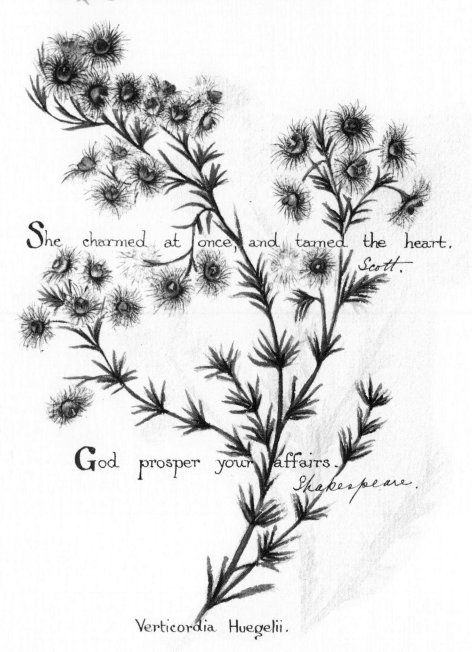

She charmed at once, and tamed the heart.
Scott.

God prosper your affairs.
Shakespeare.

Verticordia Huegelii.

23

24

25

26

November

She has the neatest little foot, and the softest little voice, and the pleasantest little smile, and the tidiest little curls, and the brightest little eyes, and the quietest little manner, and is in short, altogether one of the most engaging of all little women, dead or alive.

Dickens.

Caladenia Patersoni.

27

28

29

30

Xanthosia rotundifolia
"Southern Cross"

December

1

2

3

And all hearts do pray "God love her!" —

Aye, and certes, in good sooth,

Caladenia saccharata

We may all be sure He doth

Mr Browning.

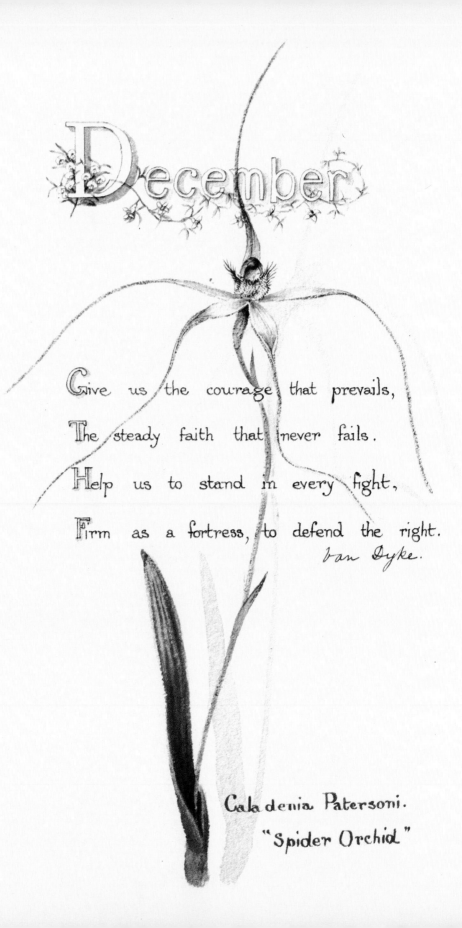

December

Give us the courage that prevails,

The steady faith that never fails.

Help us to stand in every fight,

Firm as a fortress, to defend the right.

van Dyke.

Caladenia Patersoni.

"Spider Orchid"

4

December

The soul of music slumbers in the shell,

Till waked and kindled by the masters spell;

And feeling hearts—touch them but rightly—pour

A thousand melodies unheard before.

Rogers.

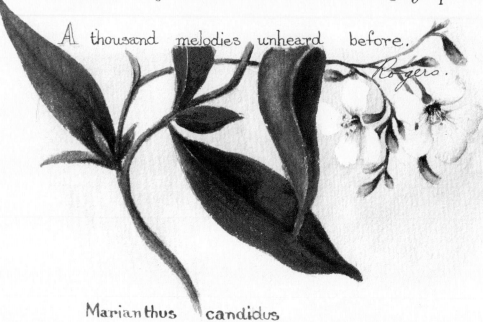

Marianthus candidus

9

10

11

12

December

"Do the good and not the clever;

Fill thy life with true endeavour;

Strive to be the noblest man,

Not what others do, but rather

Do the best you can."

Athrixia australis.

13

14

15

16

Trichocline scapigera,

18

19

To hide her cares her only art;

Her pleasure, pleasures to impart.

Pterostylis reflexa   gray

December

A kindly word and a kindly deed,

A helpful hand in time of need,

With a strong true heart to do his part,

Feeling for others, bearing their pain,

Freeing the fetters, undoing the chain.

Robert Loneman.

Isotoma Brownii

20

21

22

23

December

I heard the bells on Christmas Day

Their old, familiar carols play,

And wild and sweet

The words repeat

Of peace on earth, good-will to men!

Longfellow.

It is impossible for anyone to see her,

without being deeply interested by the

ingenuity, liveliness, and sweetness of

her disposition. —

Scott.

Acacia diptera.

24

25

26

27

December

One who in life, where'er he moved,

Drew after him the hearts of many.
Moore.

Do the work thats nearest,

Tho' it's dull at whiles,

Helping when you meet them

Lame dogs over stiles.

Actinotus leucocephalus   "Flannel Flower"

28

29

30

31

Cephalotus follicularis.

" Pitcher plant."